The Heart

J♥URNAL

of Adoption

Published by
SugarBrooke Creative Services
McIntosh, Minnesota 56556
www.sugarbrookecreative.com
(701) 361-1368

Design by Katie Krogstad

ISBN-13: 978-0-9826515-1-3

Printed in the United States of America

The Companion Journal to:

LOVE YOU BIG:

The Heart Journey of Adoption

*"And I will fill this house with glory says the Lord of hosts...
and in this place I will give peace..." Haggai 2:7-9*

"Every good and perfect gift is from above, coming down from the Father of lights..."
James 1:17

"I will put my trust in Him; here am I and the children God has given me." Hebrews 2:

"Be still and know that I am God." Psalm 46:10

"Conduct yourselves reverently during your sojourn in a strange land." 1 Peter 1:17

"Before I formed you in the womb, I knew you." Jeremiah 1:5

"For I tell you that out of these stones, God can raise up children for Abraham." Luke 3

"The man with two tunics should share with him who has none, and the one who has food should do the same." Luke 3:11

*"Now to Him who is able to do immeasurably more than all we ask or imagine...
to him be the glory in Christ Jesus throughout all generations..." Ephesians 3:20-21*

"Be anxious for nothing, but in everything by prayer and supplication, with thanksgiving, let your requests be made known to God." Philippians 4:6

*"For I know the plans I have for you, declares the Lord...
plans to give you a hope and a future."* Jeremiah 29:9

"I have called you by name...you are mine." Isaiah 43:1

"I will not leave you orphaned; I will come back to you." *John 14:18*

"Whoever welcomes one of these children in my name welcomes me; and whoever welcomes me does not welcome me but the one who sent me." Mark 9:37

*"And I will fill this house with glory says the Lord of hosts...
and in this place I will give peace..."* Haggai 2:7-9

"Every good and perfect gift is from above, coming down from the Father of lights..."
James 1:17

"I will put my trust in Him; here am I and the children God has given me." Hebrews 2:

"Be still and know that I am God." Psalm 46:10

"Conduct yourselves reverently during your sojourn in a strange land." 1 Peter 1:17

"Before I formed you in the womb, I knew you." Jeremiah 1:5

"For I tell you that out of these stones, God can raise up children for Abraham." Luke ;

"The man with two tunics should share with him who has none, and the one who has food should do the same." Luke 3:11

*"Now to Him who is able to do immeasurably more than all we ask or imagine...
to him be the glory in Christ Jesus throughout all generations..." Ephesians 3:20-21*

"Be anxious for nothing, but in everything by prayer and supplication, with thanksgiving, let your requests be made known to God." Philippians 4:6

*"For I know the plans I have for you, declares the Lord...
plans to give you a hope and a future."* Jeremiah 29:9

"I have called you by name...you are mine." Isaiah 43:1

"I will not leave you orphaned; I will come back to you." John 14:18

"Whoever welcomes one of these children in my name welcomes me; and whoever welcomes me does not welcome me but the one who sent me." Mark 9:37

"And I will fill this house with glory says the Lord of hosts...
and in this place I will give peace..." Haggai 2:7-9

"Every good and perfect gift is from above, coming down from the Father of lights..."
James 1:17

"I will put my trust in Him; here am I and the children God has given me." Hebrews 2:

"Be still and know that I am God." Psalm 46:10

"Conduct yourselves reverently during your sojourn in a strange land." 1 Peter 1:17

"Before I formed you in the womb, I knew you." Jeremiah 1:5

"For I tell you that out of these stones, God can raise up children for Abraham." Luke 3

"The man with two tunics should share with him who has none, and the one who has food should do the same." Luke 3:11

*"Now to Him who is able to do immeasurably more than all we ask or imagine...
to him be the glory in Christ Jesus throughout all generations..." Ephesians 3:20-21*

"Be anxious for nothing, but in everything by prayer and supplication, with thanksgiving, let your requests be made known to God." Philippians 4:6

"For I know the plans I have for you, declares the Lord...
plans to give you a hope and a future." Jeremiah 29:9

"I have called you by name...you are mine." Isaiah 43:1

"I will not leave you orphaned; I will come back to you." John 14:18

"Whoever welcomes one of these children in my name welcomes me; and whoever welcomes me does not welcome me but the one who sent me." Mark 9:37

*"And I will fill this house with glory says the Lord of hosts...
and in this place I will give peace..." Haggai 2:7-9*

"Every good and perfect gift is from above, coming down from the Father of lights..."
James 1:17

"I will put my trust in Him; here am I and the children God has given me." Hebrews 2:

"Be still and know that I am God." Psalm 46:10

"Conduct yourselves reverently during your sojourn in a strange land." 1 Peter 1:17

"Before I formed you in the womb, I knew you." Jeremiah 1:5

"For I tell you that out of these stones, God can raise up children for Abraham." Luke

*"The man with two tunics should share with him who has none,
and the one who has food should do the same."* Luke 3:11

*"Now to Him who is able to do immeasurably more than all we ask or imagine...
to him be the glory in Christ Jesus throughout all generations..." Ephesians 3:20-21*

"Be anxious for nothing, but in everything by prayer and supplication, with thanksgiving, let your requests be made known to God." Philippians 4:6

"For I know the plans I have for you, declares the Lord...
plans to give you a hope and a future." Jeremiah 29:9

"I have called you by name...you are mine." Isaiah 43:1

"I will not leave you orphaned; I will come back to you." John 14:18

"Whoever welcomes one of these children in my name welcomes me; and whoever welcomes me does not welcome me but the one who sent me." Mark 9:37

*"And I will fill this house with glory says the Lord of hosts...
and in this place I will give peace..."* *Haggai 2:7-9*

"Every good and perfect gift is from above, coming down from the Father of lights..."
James 1:17

"I will put my trust in Him; here am I and the children God has given me." Hebrews 2:

"Be still and know that I am God." Psalm 46:10

"Conduct yourselves reverently during your sojourn in a strange land." 1 Peter 1:17

"Before I formed you in the womb, I knew you." Jeremiah 1:5

"For I tell you that out of these stones, God can raise up children for Abraham." Luke

"The man with two tunics should share with him who has none, and the one who has food should do the same." Luke 3:11

*"Now to Him who is able to do immeasurably more than all we ask or imagine...
to him be the glory in Christ Jesus throughout all generations..."* Ephesians 3:20-21

"Be anxious for nothing, but in everything by prayer and supplication, with thanksgiving, let your requests be made known to God." Philippians 4:6

*"For I know the plans I have for you, declares the Lord...
plans to give you a hope and a future."* Jeremiah 29:9

"I have called you by name...you are mine." Isaiah 43:1

"I will not leave you orphaned; I will come back to you." John 14:18

"Whoever welcomes one of these children in my name welcomes me; and whoever welcomes me does not welcome me but the one who sent me." Mark 9:37

*"And I will fill this house with glory says the Lord of hosts...
and in this place I will give peace..." Haggai 2:7-9*

"Every good and perfect gift is from above, coming down from the Father of lights..."
James 1:17

"I will put my trust in Him; here am I and the children God has given me." Hebrews 2:

"Be still and know that I am God." Psalm 46:10

"Conduct yourselves reverently during your sojourn in a strange land." 1 Peter 1:17

"Before I formed you in the womb, I knew you." Jeremiah 1:5

"For I tell you that out of these stones, God can raise up children for Abraham." Luke 3

*"The man with two tunics should share with him who has none,
and the one who has food should do the same." Luke 3:11*

"Now to Him who is able to do immeasurably more than all we ask or imagine... to him be the glory in Christ Jesus throughout all generations..." Ephesians 3:20-21

"Be anxious for nothing, but in everything by prayer and supplication, with thanksgiving, let your requests be made known to God." Philippians 4:6

"For I know the plans I have for you, declares the Lord...
plans to give you a hope and a future." Jeremiah 29:9

"I have called you by name...you are mine." Isaiah 43:1

"I will not leave you orphaned; I will come back to you." John 14:18

"Whoever welcomes one of these children in my name welcomes me; and whoever welcomes me does not welcome me but the one who sent me." Mark 9:37

*"And I will fill this house with glory says the Lord of hosts...
and in this place I will give peace..."* Haggai 2:7-9

"Every good and perfect gift is from above, coming down from the Father of lights..."
James 1:17

"I will put my trust in Him; here am I and the children God has given me." Hebrews 2:

"Be still and know that I am God." Psalm 46:10

"Conduct yourselves reverently during your sojourn in a strange land." 1 Peter 1:17

"Before I formed you in the womb, I knew you." Jeremiah 1:5

"For I tell you that out of these stones, God can raise up children for Abraham." Luke

"The man with two tunics should share with him who has none, and the one who has food should do the same." Luke 3:11

*"Now to Him who is able to do immeasurably more than all we ask or imagine...
to him be the glory in Christ Jesus throughout all generations..."* Ephesians 3:20-21

"Be anxious for nothing, but in everything by prayer and supplication, with thanksgiving, let your requests be made known to God." Philippians 4:6

"For I know the plans I have for you, declares the Lord...
plans to give you a hope and a future." Jeremiah 29:9

"I have called you by name...you are mine." Isaiah 43:1

"I will not leave you orphaned; I will come back to you." John 14:18

"Whoever welcomes one of these children in my name welcomes me; and whoever welcomes me does not welcome me but the one who sent me." Mark 9:37

"Every good and perfect gift is from above, coming down from the Father of lights..."
James 1:17

"I will put my trust in Him; here am I and the children God has given me." Hebrews 2:

"Be still and know that I am God." Psalm 46:10

"Conduct yourselves reverently during your sojourn in a strange land." 1 Peter 1:17

"Before I formed you in the womb, I knew you." Jeremiah 1:5

"For I tell you that out of these stones, God can raise up children for Abraham." Luke :

"The man with two tunics should share with him who has none,
and the one who has food should do the same." Luke 3:11

*"Now to Him who is able to do immeasurably more than all we ask or imagine...
to him be the glory in Christ Jesus throughout all generations..." Ephesians 3:20-21*

"Be anxious for nothing, but in everything by prayer and supplication, with thanksgiving, let your requests be made known to God." Philippians 4:6

*"For I know the plans I have for you, declares the Lord...
plans to give you a hope and a future."* Jeremiah 29:9

"I have called you by name...you are mine." Isaiah 43:1

"I will not leave you orphaned; I will come back to you." John 14:18

"Whoever welcomes one of these children in my name welcomes me; and whoever welcomes me does not welcome me but the one who sent me." Mark 9:37

"And I will fill this house with glory says the Lord of hosts…
and in this place I will give peace…" Haggai 2:7-9

"Every good and perfect gift is from above, coming down from the Father of lights..."
James 1:17

"I will put my trust in Him; here am I and the children God has given me." Hebrews 2:

"Be still and know that I am God." Psalm 46:10

"*Conduct yourselves reverently during your sojourn in a strange land.*" 1 Peter 1:17

"Before I formed you in the womb, I knew you." Jeremiah 1:5

"For I tell you that out of these stones, God can raise up children for Abraham." Luke .

*"The man with two tunics should share with him who has none,
and the one who has food should do the same." Luke 3:11*

*"Now to Him who is able to do immeasurably more than all we ask or imagine...
to him be the glory in Christ Jesus throughout all generations..." Ephesians 3:20-21*

"Be anxious for nothing, but in everything by prayer and supplication, with thanksgiving, let your requests be made known to God." Philippians 4:6

God bless your very own heart journey!